HAL LEONARD GUITAR METHOD

LAP STEEL GUITAR

BY JOHNIE HELMS

To access audio visit:
www.halleonard.com/mylibrary

Enter Code
5866-7093-8025-1433

ISBN 978-1-4234-2270-9

HAL•LEONARD®
CORPORATION

7777 W. BLUEMOUND RD. P.O. BOX 13819 MILWAUKEE, WI 53213

In Australia Contact:
Hal Leonard Australia Pty. Ltd.
4 Lentara Court
Cheltenham, Victoria, 3192 Australia
Email: ausadmin@halleonard.com.au

Visit Hal Leonard Online at
www.halleonard.com

ABOUT THE AUTHOR

Johnie Helms comes from a musical family and started on standard guitar at age twelve. During high school, Johnie played bass guitar for several bands, usually three nights a week, at area clubs.

Johnie has toured professionally for over 18 years, playing both pedal steel and slide guitar for many famous country artists both old and new. His longest was a ten-year stint with country superstar Toby Keith. He has also played on over 700 recording sessions to date and has an instrumental CD of his own.

Johnie has appeared on numerous television shows such as Austin City Limits, ABC Spring Break, the Academy of Country Music Awards, CBS Early Show, and the Country Music Awards. In 2002, he was nominated as instrumentalist of the year in the pedal steel guitar category by the Academy of Country Music.

He is also the author of the *Hal Leonard Pedal Steel Method*.

ACKNOWLEDGMENTS

Thanks for the support and assistance of my family, Ty England, Ken Collins, Gibson/Epiphone, Peavey Electronics, Sound Tech-Washburn, Crate/Alvarez, and Eminence Speakers.

Johnie dedicates this book to his father, George Helms, and Vernon Page, for sharing their love for and knowledge of the steel guitar and being his mentors and inspiration.

Photography by Gary England.

A BRIEF HISTORY

Although the actual origins of the Hawaiian lap steel guitar may never be known for sure, most have accredited a young man named Joseph KeKuKu around the year 1885. As the story goes, he picked up a metal bolt lying by a railroad track and began experimenting with the technique of sliding a metal bar along the guitar's strings to change the pitch of individual notes.

The popularity of Hawaiian steel guitar music made the instrument a mainstay in the early 1900s. Soon to follow was the country music industry, which welcomed the unique tones derived from the lap steel guitar. Even though the lap steel began losing popularity somewhere around the 1960s, thanks to the invention of the pedal steel guitar, it is currently experiencing resurgence, thanks in part to the "slide guitar style" that is common to country, rock, and pop music—not to forget the joyous sounds of the "sacred steel" so popular in House of God congregations.

INTRODUCTION TO THE LAP STEEL

The lap steel guitar has been attracting musicians and listeners for more than a hundred years in practically every style of music imaginable. Lap steels come in a variety of sizes and shapes, and can be found as six-, eight-, ten-, and sometimes twelve-string models. This book will be dealing with the basic six-string model.

The term "lap steel" will be used in this book to refer to any non-pedal acoustic or electric steel guitar that is played flat on the player's lap or on a stand. Many of the tunings and licks covered in this book could also be played on standard guitar using a slide on one finger.

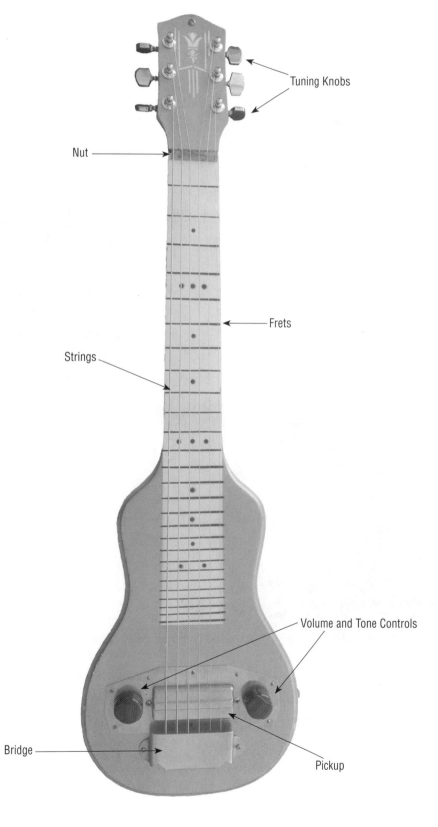

Tuning Knobs

Nut

Frets

Strings

Volume and Tone Controls

Bridge

Pickup

ACCESSORIES AND NECESSITIES

Pictured below are some of the items you'll need to properly tune, play, and amplify your lap steel guitar.

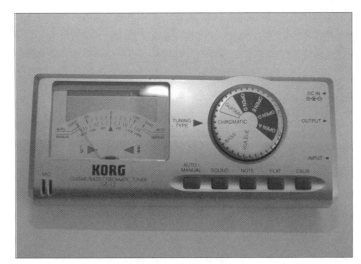

Electronic Tuner

Guitar Amplifier

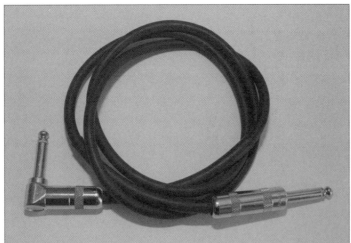

Guitar Cable

PICKS

Start by placing the thumb pick on your thumb and a pick on both the index and middle fingers. Finger picks should be worn with the band across the fingernail and the tip bent back slightly towards your fingertip.

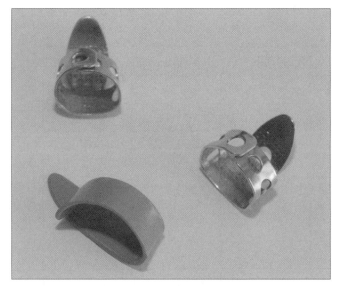

Thumb Pick and Two Finger Picks

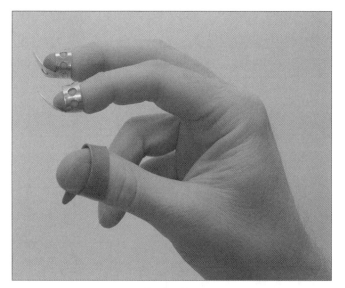

Wearing Picks

THE BAR

Although many lap steel players use the "pedal steel" bullet bar…

Pedal Steel (Bullet) Bar

…the "grooved" lap steel or dobro-style bar is recommended. It is easier to grip and allows for better accuracy for hammer-ons and pull-offs. (We'll introduce those techniques later.)

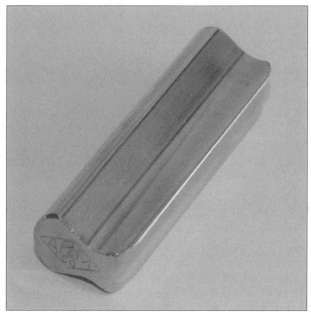

Lap Steel Bar

LAP STEEL GUITAR TUNINGS

In this book we will be using four basic lap steel tunings: open G, open D, open A, and open E. These will be introduced as they appear. Some of the many different tunings to choose from are listed here.

Tuning	String 1	String 2	String 3	String 4	String 5	String 6
C6	E	C	A	G	E	C
E major	E	B	G#	E	B	E
G major	D	B	G	D	G	D
G6	D	B	G	E	B	G
A major	E	C#	A	E	C#	A
A6	E	C#	A	F#	E	C#
D major	D	A	F#	D	A	D
E7	E	B	G#	E	D	B

Many players thoughout the years have spent long hours searching for the ultimate tuning. It may be best to narrow the search to a few basic tunings that suit your playing style and situation. For example, the 6th tunings are often preferred for jazz and Western swing styles, while the major and 7th (dominant) tunings work well for blues and rock.

OPEN G TUNING

Our first exercises and songs will be in **open G tuning** (or **G major tuning**, as listed above). Track 1 plays the notes of the open strings of the guitar in this tuning, starting on the first string and working back to the sixth. You can either use this track to tune your lap steel, or use an electronic tuner.

 OPEN G TUNING

TRACK 1

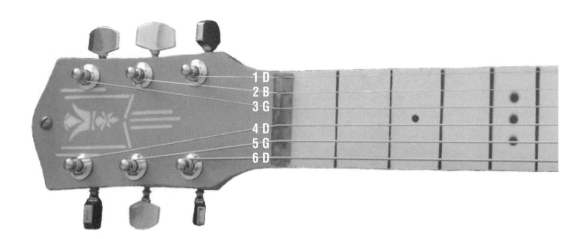

If you're tuning a string that is **sharp** (too high in pitch), it's best to loosen it until it is lower than the target note, then bring it up to pitch. This stabilizes the string tension and helps the string stay in tune longer.

STRING GAUGES

String gauge is of special significance to all lap steel players. Some prefer a more "loose" feeling string (light gauge), while others favor strings with a much "tighter" feel (heavy gauge).

Another factor to consider when choosing strings is the guitar's scale length. The tension on a long-scale instrument is noticeably greater when the strings are brought up to pitch, necessitating the use of light-gauge strings. A smaller, standard lap steel guitar would benefit from a much heavier set.

Finally, the tuning you use largely determines your string gauge. The chart below will give you some idea of the gauges for a few tunings and should be used as a general guideline.

Tuning	String 1	String 2	String 3	String 4	String 5	String 6
C6	E 12–15	C 16–18	A 20–22	G 24–26	E 28–32	C 34–38
E major	E 12–15	B 17–19	G# 24–26	E 28–32	B 34–38	E 54–58
G major	D 15–17	B 17–19	G 24–26	D 32–36	G 44–48	D 60–64
A major	E 12–15	C# 16–18	A 20–22	E 28–32	C# 34–38	A 40–44
D major	D 15–17	A 20–22	F# 24–26	D 32–36	A 40–44	D 60–64
E7	E 12–15	B 17–19	G# 24–26	E 28–32	D 32–36	B 34–38

POSTURE

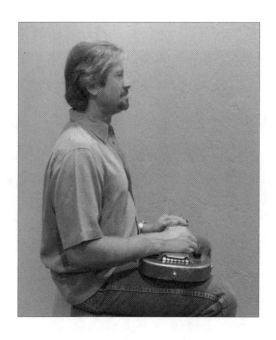

Start in a comfortable sitting position with your knees bent and your feet flat on the ground. Place the guitar on your lap in a manner that will allow you the best visibility of the playing surface.

You may need to adjust the height of your chair so the guitar lies flat on your lap.

RIGHT- AND LEFT-HAND TECHNIQUE

THE PICKING HAND

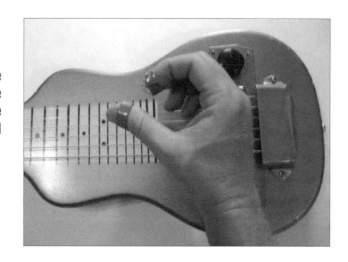

Note that this method is written for right-handed players. If you are left-handed, simply reverse the given directions. Start by placing the edge of your right hand on top of the strings to the left of the **bridge** (the metal piece where the strings end). If you make a loose, relaxed fist, you'll notice your fingers are curved back toward you.

Roll your right hand toward the strings to the point where, as you look down at your hand, you see the knuckles of the index and middle fingers. The edge of your palm should now be off the strings, but fairly close to them.

This is a good starting point for the right hand. Not all steel guitar players have the same technique and it is important that you develop a technique that is comfortable for you.

HOLDING THE LAP STEEL BAR

Start by laying your index finger in the top groove, then place your thumb and middle finger along the front and back grooves of the bar. Now place the bar directly above the fret, with the bottom "rounded" part of the bar on the strings, allowing your ring and pinky fingers to rest on the strings behind the bar. Note that lap steel guitars don't have actual frets like a regular guitar, but lines that represent frets. These can help you see exactly where to align your bar so you can play in tune.

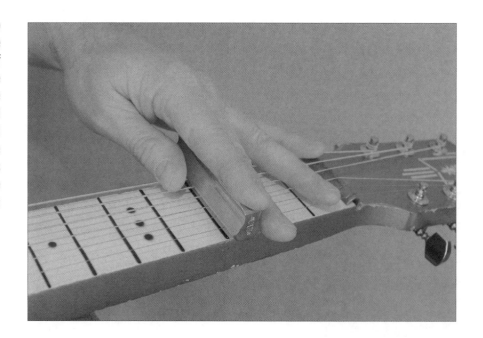

TABLATURE

In music diagrammed for lap steel guitar, there are spaces that represent each string.

The diagram below has four figures that illustrate the tablature for most of the playing moves you'll encounter.

1. In figure 1, the first column of the diagram, the spaces numbered 1 to 6 on the left side of the page indicate the string numbers. String 1 is the highest and 6 is the lowest.

2. In figure 2, the second column, the fret where the bar is placed is indicated by a number located within a space. Even though the frets aren't actually played like a standard guitar, they are used as markers for bar position.

3. In figure 3 we see the notes aligned vertically; these should be played together.

4. Figure 4 shows a dotted line between notes (sometimes an arched line is used). This means that the bar is slid to another position without picking the notes on the right-hand side of the line. In this case, the seventh-fret notes are picked on strings 3 and 4, then the bar is slid to fret 9.

Figure 1	Figure 2	Figure 3	Figure 4
1			
2			
3	2	2	7 - - - - - 9
4		2	7 - - - - - 9
5			
6			

MUSIC NOTATION

This book uses **standard notation** along with the lap steel tablature, as described above. See the Appendix in the back of the book for the basics of standard notation. Though you can play the music in this method with the tablature and CD alone, it is highly recommended that you learn to read music.

SCALES

A **scale** is a series of consecutive musical tones. An **interval** is the distance between any two tones. Scales are defined by the order of intervals between the tones. Listed in this book are several basic scales within the different tunings available.

The main reason for learning these scales is to be able to use individual notes within the scale to create licks and runs, and also to be able to **ad-lib** (or improvise) a solo. Plus, when you know a song is in a particular key—in this case, G major—you know that all or most of the notes in that song will be derived from the G major scale.

MAJOR SCALE

A **major scale** contains five whole steps and two half steps, with the half steps between the 3rd and 4th, and between the 7th and 8th tones. The major scale represents the basic building blocks of Western music.

 Play along with track 2: the **G major scale** in open G tuning.

TRACK 2

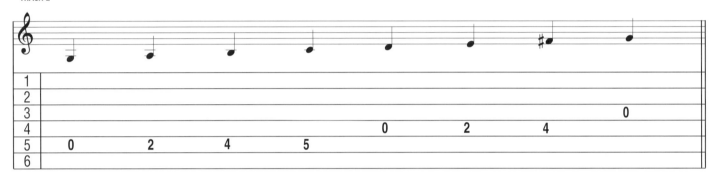

 Track 3 is the G major scale an octave higher.

TRACK 3

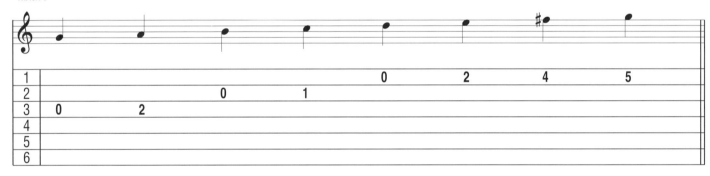

 Track 4 covers both octaves of the G major scale.

TRACK 4

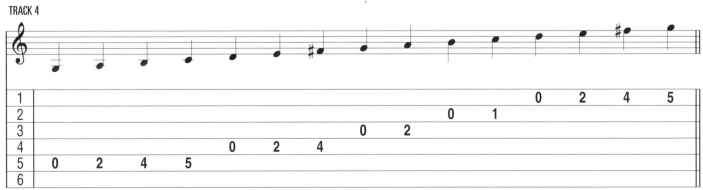

CHORDS IN THE KEY OF G

BASIC MAJOR CHORDS

The basic **major chords**, or **major triads**, consist of three notes: a root, 3rd, and 5th. These notes are the first, 3rd, and 5th degrees of the major scale. For example, if we build a major chord based on the notes of the C major scale: C D E F G A B C, then we would have a C major chord with the notes C, E, and G.

In open G tuning, the open strings form a G major chord with the notes G (the root), B (the 3rd), and D (the 5th) repeated in different orders. This makes it easy to play major chords all over the neck with a straight bar over each fret. Here's a chart of every chord at every fret in open G tuning:

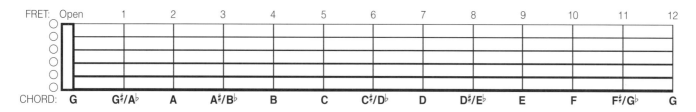

KEY POSITIONS

Here's how you can quickly find the standard chords commonly found within a song from its respective key. The most basic are referred to as the I, IV, and V chords. They're based on the first, fourth, and fifth notes of a major scale. In the key of G, those chords are as follows:

TRACK 5

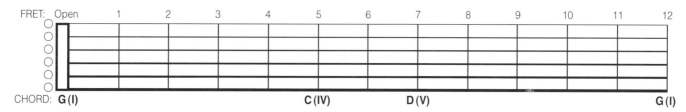

To this formula we can add the minor vi chord, which has a flatted 3rd. On lap steel, we can simply omit the 3rd by not playing that note. You can do this by placing a finger over the second string to keep it from sounding as you play the E minor chord at fret 9.

TRACK 6

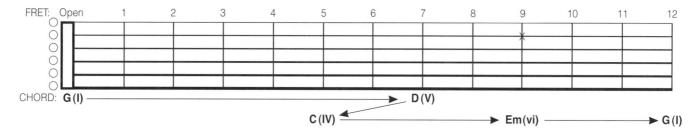

BLOCKING

Blocking is when the vibrations of strings are **damped** to stop them from making unwanted sounds. The two types of blocking covered here are **palm blocking** with the right hand and **left-hand blocking**.

PALM BLOCKING

Palm blocking involves using the edge of your right hand, or picking hand, to damp the string (silence its vibration). Lift your hand up slightly while you play the note, then place the edge of your hand back down to damp the note. Check out audio track 7.

TRACK 7

LEFT-HAND BLOCKING

Left-hand blocking involves lifting your bar and allowing your two remaining left-hand fingers to damp the strings by simply resting on the strings. This technique is much easier to do with a lap steel bar, as opposed to the standard pedal steel bar. Hear it in action on track 8.

TRACK 8

A good blocking exercise for either style is demonstrated on audio track 9.

TRACK 9

String	Finger
1	I
2	T
3	I
4	T
5	I
6	T

With the bar at fret 5, start by picking the first string with your index finger (I), then pick string 2 with your thumb (T). Alternate between the finger and thumb all the way to string 6, then work your way back from string 6 to string 1. Try left-hand and palm blocking here as well.

String	Finger
1	M
2	T
3	M
4	T
5	M
6	T

Once you have completed the exercise, go back and play it using the middle finger (M) in place of the index finger.

KEY SIGNATURES

In music notation, the G major scale always has a sharp note: F♯. Rather than writing the sharps or flats every time they occur, we use a **key signature** at the beginning of the notation.

A complete study of key signatures is beyond the scope of a beginner's book. Right now, it's all about learning to play—so let's learn a song!

GRACE NOTES

Many lap steel licks make extensive use of **grace notes**. Usually they're played by picking a note and then immediately sliding into the "real" note, producing that distinctive lap steel sliding sound. In tablature, grace notes look like any other note, but on the staff they are smaller and have a slash through them to signify that theoretically they don't take up any time in the music notation. Slides are shown with a dashed line in the tablature, and a solid line in the standard notation staff.

"Midnight Special" is in the key of G and includes slides and blocking.

MIDNIGHT SPECIAL

TRACK 10
with lap guitar

TRACK 11
rhythm track

THE BAR BOUNCE

The **bar bounce** is a technique that involves setting down and lifting up the bar to get quick note changes. There are certain types of uses for this technique, as follows:

The **hammer-on**: This technique is used to move from a lower note to a higher one—often from an open string to a fretted note.

TRACK 12

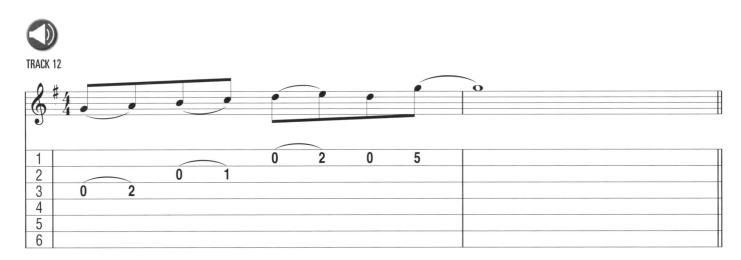

The **pull-off** is used to move from a higher note to a lower note, also used often in open-string playing situations.

TRACK 13

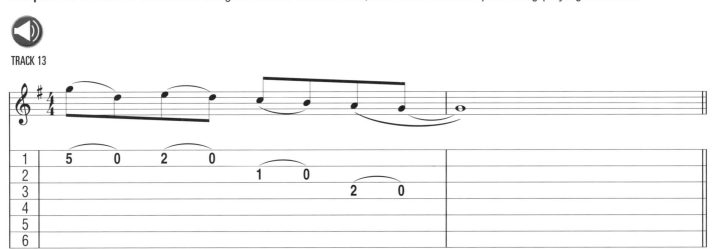

REPEAT SIGNS

When a section of music is played twice in a row, we use **repeat signs** instead of writing it out a second time. When you get to the left-facing repeat sign (:‖), go back to the right-facing repeat sign (‖:) and play the section again. Try this in "Down in the Valley."

"Down in the Valley" is in a **3/4 time signature**. Each measure has three beats, and a quarter note gets one beat. Count, "One–two–three, One–two–three…"

TRACK 14
with lap guitar

TRACK 15
rhythm track

DOWN IN THE VALLEY

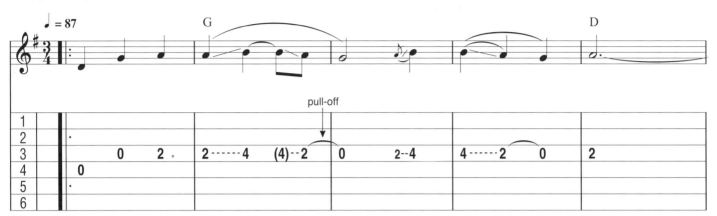

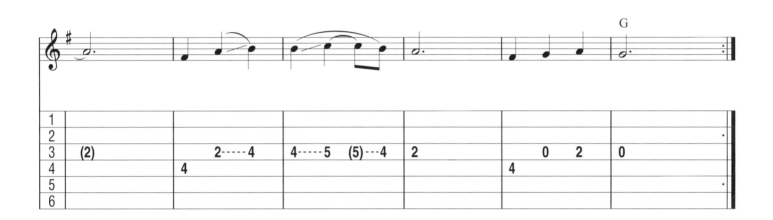

PICKUP NOTES

Music doesn't always begin on beat 1. When you begin after beat 1, the notes before the first full measure are called **pickup notes**.

"Go, Tell It on the Mountain" is played with a pattern that repeats, but it ends slightly different the second time. **First and second endings** are used to show this. Play through the song until you reach the repeat sign, then go back and play it from the right-facing repeat. But this time, skip the first ending (labeled with a bracket and the number one) and play the second ending that is labeled with a bracket and the number two.

TRACK 16
with lap guitar

TRACK 17
rhythm track

GO, TELL IT ON THE MOUNTAIN

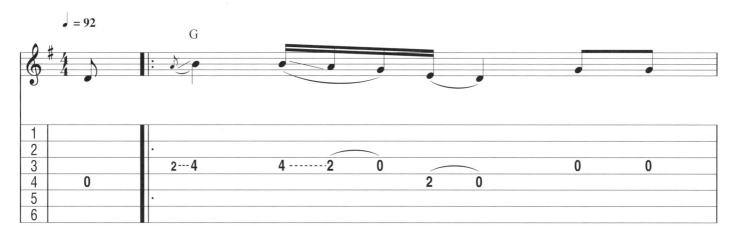

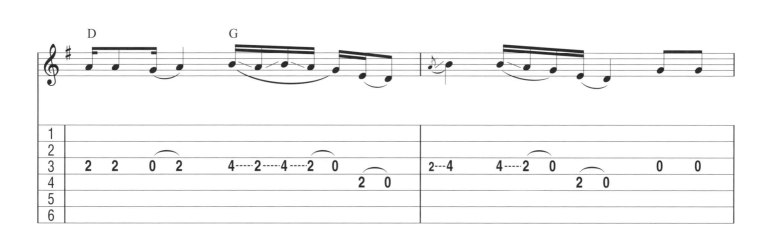

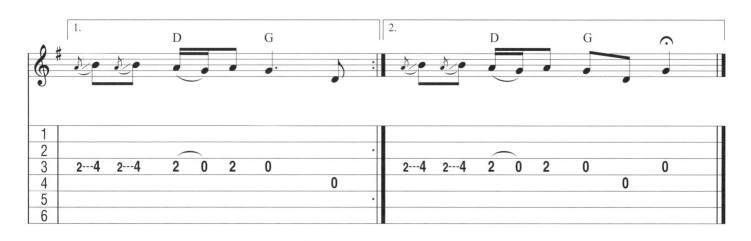

VIBRATO

Vibrato is the slight fluctuation a note's pitch. You will need to develop slow, medium, and fast vibrato. The decision about which is appropriate at a given time depends on the song. Vibrato is especially necessary for helping the lap steel guitar sound in tune, because it has no actual frets—only fret markers.

Start by placing your bar at the fifth fret. Pick the second string and roll the bar back and forth slightly. Some people sweep the bar in a mild circular motion, but most use the rolling method.

When we read tablature and notation, vibrato is depicted with a squiggly line: ～～～～

TRACK 18

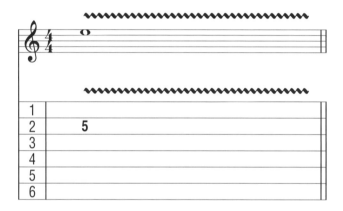

Here is an example of a faster vibrato style, suitable for a rock 'n' roll song:

TRACK 19

PRACTICE TIP

Regular practice is essential. Practicing a half hour every day is better than practicing two hours every four days. Find a regular time that works for you.

"Amazing Grace" is in 3/4 time and begins with a pickup note on beat 3.

AMAZING GRACE

MORE TECHNIQUES

SLANTS

The **bar slant** technique is used to play two or three notes that are not on the same fret. Slants can be very difficult to master. Take your time and practice, making sure the two strings are in correct pitch with one another.

For the **forward slant**, use your fingers to move the bar with your thumb as a pivot point.

FORWARD SLANT

TRACK 22

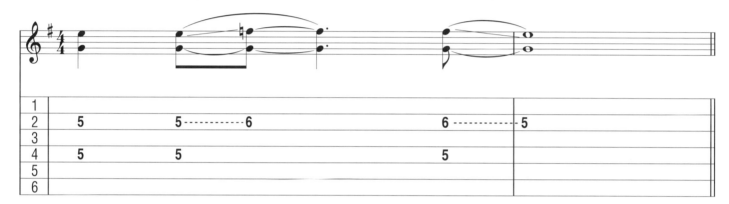

For the **reverse slant**, try moving your wrist and keeping the bar cupped in your hand.

REVERSE SLANT

TRACK 23

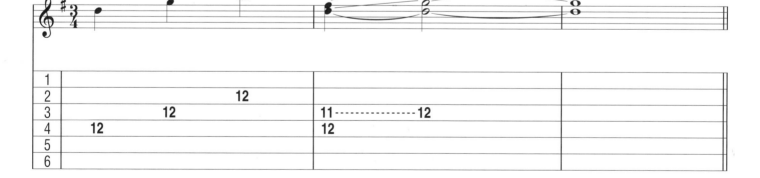

Remember, you are manually imitating the sound of a pedal steel guitar, so take your time listening to each voice.

STRING PULLS

Yet another lap steel trick, **string pulls** involve pulling or stretching a certain string from behind the bar. After you've picked the string, pull it toward you using your bar hand's ring finger, but keep the string in contact with the bar as you raise the note.

If necessary, place your bar-hand thumb against the lower string or neck of the guitar for added control. String pulls are indicated in tablature with a solid line and in standard notation with a bend symbol, or pointed slur (⌃).

EXAMPLE 1

TRACK 24

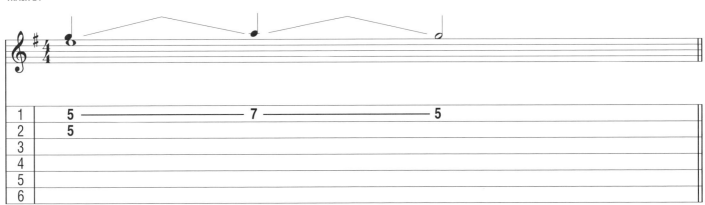

EXAMPLE 2

TRACK 25

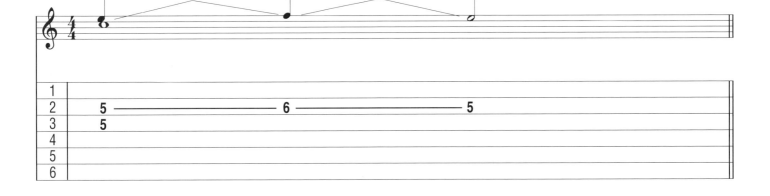

LICKS IN OPEN G

These licks for open G tuning can be used as song introductions and endings, turnarounds (usually the last two measures of a repeated song form), fills between lines or song sections, and in solos. These are in the key of G, but you could work them out in different keys and at various tempos until you can play them in any situation.

LICK 1

TRACK 26

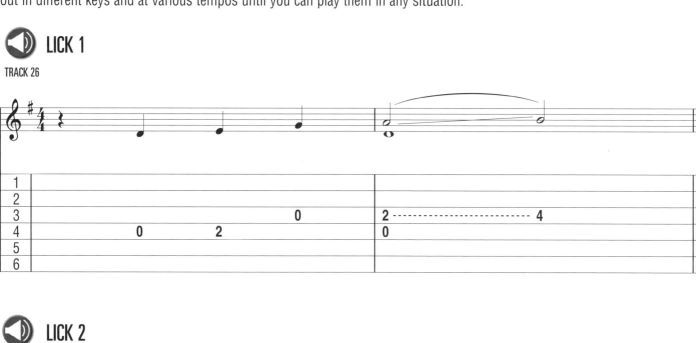

LICK 2

TRACK 27

LICK 3

TRACK 28

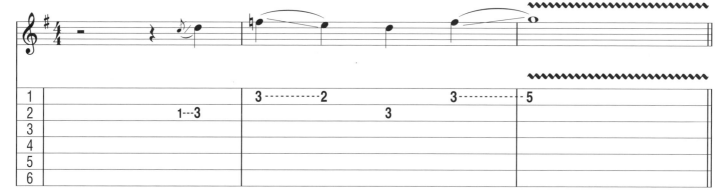

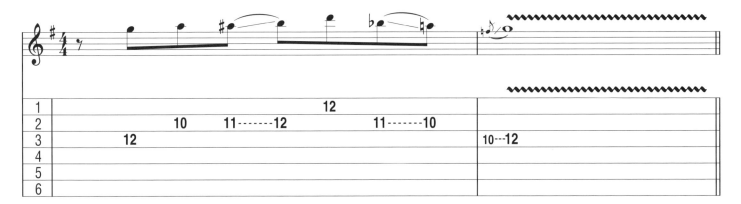

STACCATO

One result of string blocking is the playing of notes in a separated, distinct manner known as **staccato**. When a note is to be played staccato, a dot is shown directly above the notehead, as in Lick 5 below.

LICK 5

TRACK 30

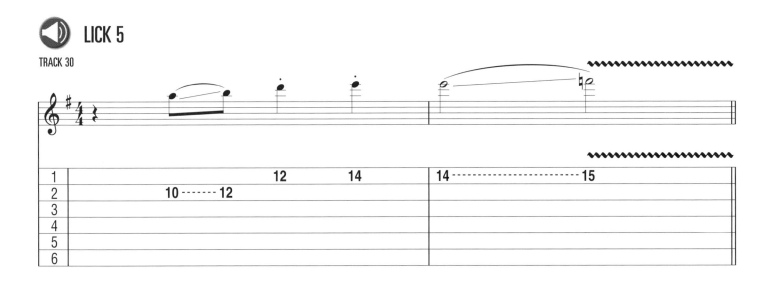

LICK 6

TRACK 31

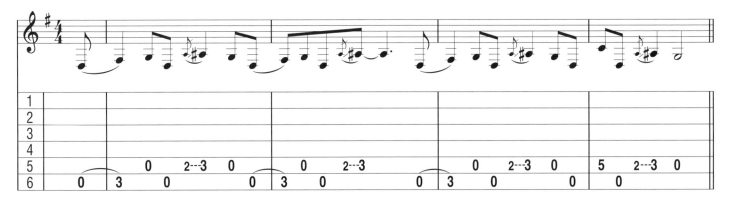

LICK 7

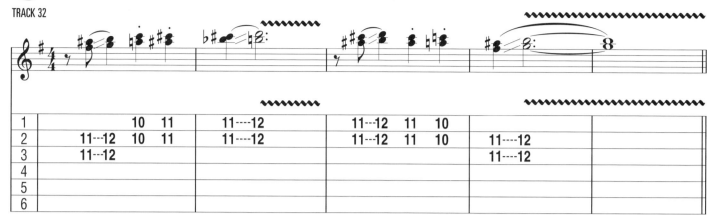

1		10 11	11----12	11--12 11 10	
2	11---12 10 11	11----12	11--12 11 10	11----12
3	11---12			11----12
4				
5				
6				

LICK 8

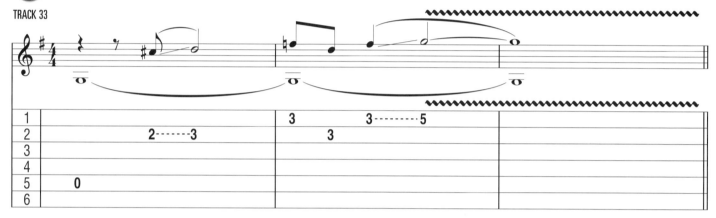

1		3 3--------5	
2	2------3	3	
3			
4			
5	0		
6			

LICK 9

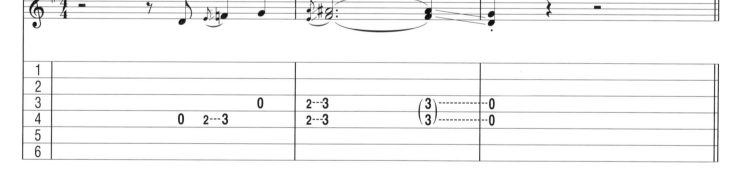

1			
2			
3	0	2--3	(3)----------0
4	0 2---3	2--3	(3)----------0
5			
6			

LICK 10

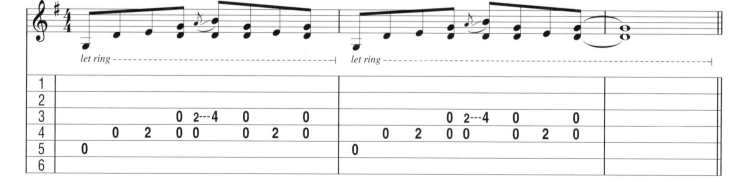

let ring ----------------------------   *let ring ----------------------------*

1			
2			
3	0 2---4 0 0	0 2---4 0 0	
4	0 2 0 0 0 2 0	0 2 0 0 0 2 0	
5	0	0	
6			

OPEN D TUNING

The strings for open D tuning are tuned as follows:

 OPEN D TUNING

TRACK 36

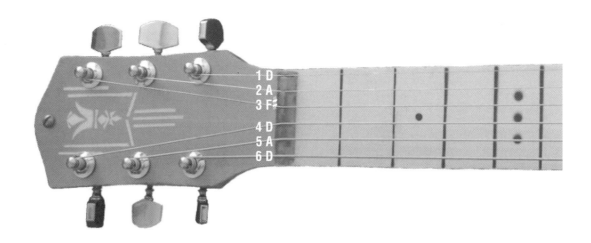

D MAJOR SCALE

 Play along with track 37: the D major scale in open D tuning.

TRACK 37

 Track 38 is the D major scale an octave higher.

TRACK 38

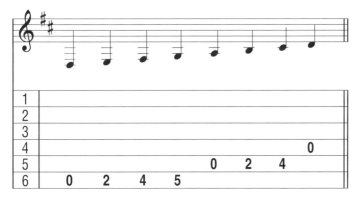

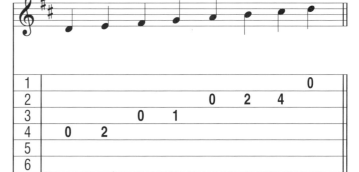

 Track 39 covers both octaves of the D major scale.

TRACK 39

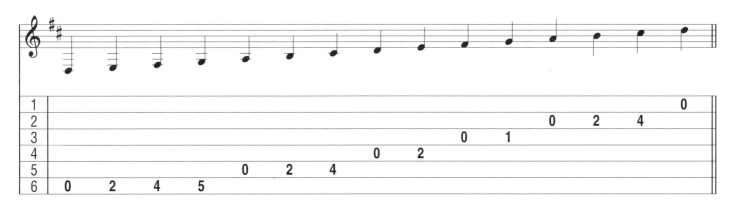

24

CHORDS IN THE KEY OF D

BASIC MAJOR CHORDS

Like open G tuning, open D tuning does just what the name implies: it forms an open D major chord with the open-string notes D (the root), F# (the 3rd), and A (the 5th). This gives you straight major chords all over the neck:

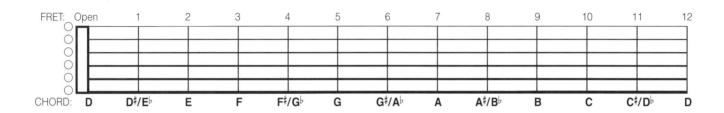

KEY POSITIONS

The I, IV, and V chords in D are D, G, and A.

TRACK 40

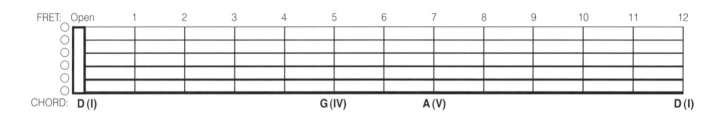

When playing the minor vi chord in the key of D, dampen the 3rd string to keep the major 3rd note from ringing as you play the B minor at fret 9.

TRACK 41

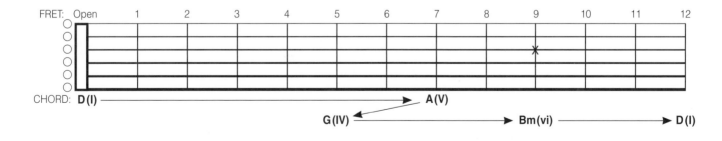

AURA LEE

TRACK 42
with steel guitar

TRACK 43
rhythm track

ARPEGGIO

An **arpeggio** is a "broken" chord whose notes are played one at a time instead of all at once. Arpeggios often show up in lap steel songs, as in "Git'n in the Mood," where the main riff is based on an **arpeggiated** D major chord.

GIT'N IN THE MOOD

TRACK 44
with steel guitar

TRACK 45
rhythm track

THE SHUFFLE

You might have noticed something different about the rhythm of "Git'n in the Mood." Its eighth notes are played unevenly, more like a heartbeat than a regular beat. This is called **shuffle** or **swing feel**, and it is symbolized at the top of the tune with a symbol in parentheses: (♫ = ♪♪). This tells you to play each pair of eighth notes as a long note followed by a short note. The shuffle is common in blues, country, jazz, and rock music.

27

LICKS IN OPEN D

Here is a collection of must-know licks in the key of D. These should also be played in different keys and tempos.

 LICK 1

TRACK 46

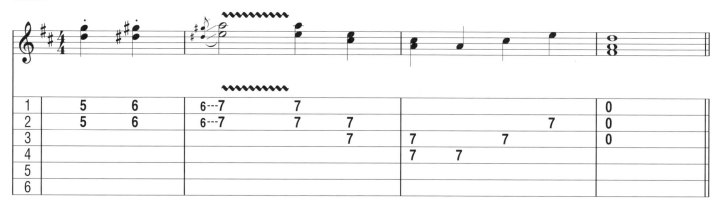

 LICK 2

TRACK 47

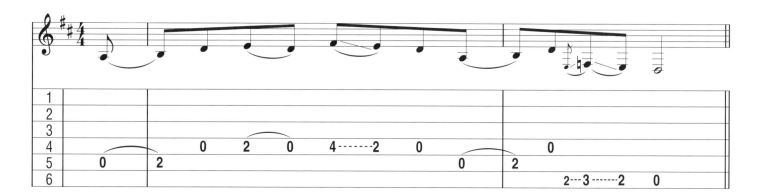

 LICK 3

TRACK 48

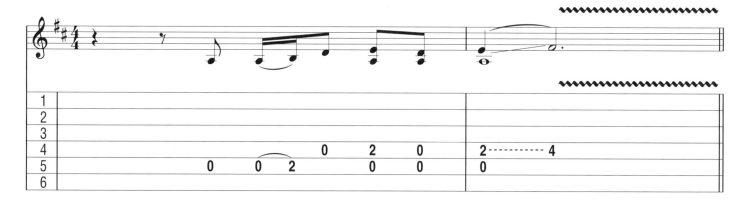

TRACK 49

LICK 4

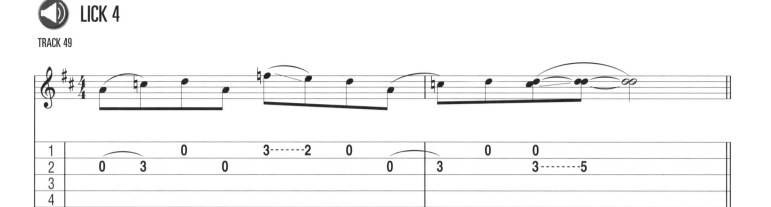

LICK 5

TRACK 50

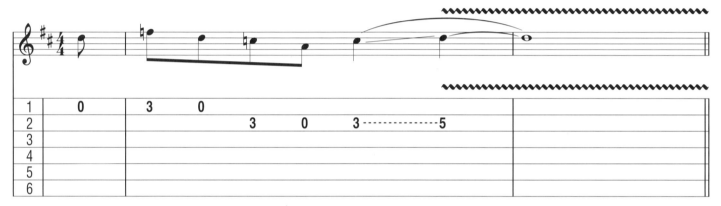

LICK 6

TRACK 51

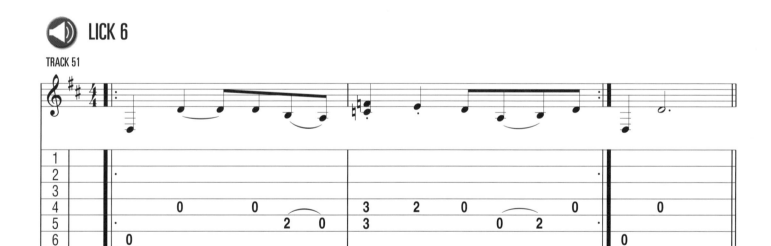

ANOTHER KIND OF ARPEGGIO

The first chord of Lick 7 is played as a **rake**, where the notes are picked as a quick arpeggio from low to high (as shown by a squiggly line with an arrow on top). "Rake" your thumb pick across the strings to get this effect.

LICK 7

TRACK 52

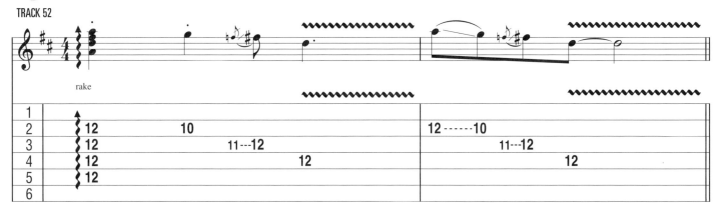

LICK 8

TRACK 53

LICK 9

TRACK 54

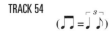

LICK 10

TRACK 55

OPEN A TUNING

Here are the open strings for open A tuning:

 OPEN A TUNING

TRACK 56

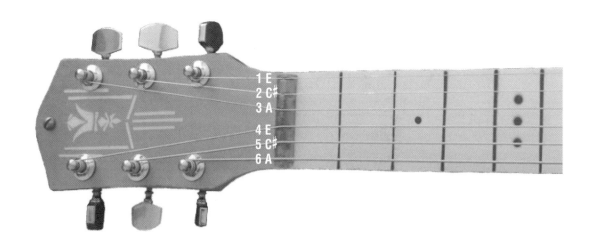

A MAJOR SCALE

 Play along with track 57: the A major scale in open A tuning.

TRACK 57

 Track 58 is the A major scale an octave higher.

TRACK 58

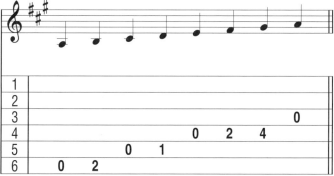

1							0
2							
3							
4					0	2	4
5		0	1				
6	0	2					

1					0	2	4	5
2				0	1			
3	0	2						
4								
5								
6								

 Track 59 covers both octaves of the A major scale.

TRACK 59

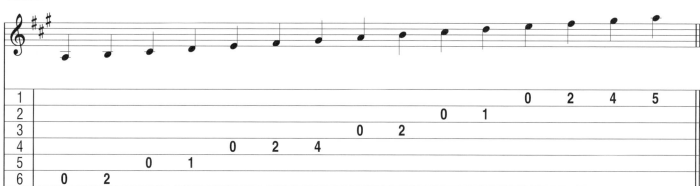

1										0	2	4	5
2								0	1				
3						0	2						
4					0	2	4						
5		0	1										
6	0	2											

CHORDS IN THE KEY OF A

BASIC MAJOR CHORDS

The open strings in open A tuning form an A major chord with the notes A (the root), C# (the 3rd), and E (the 5th). This produces the following major chords across the neck:

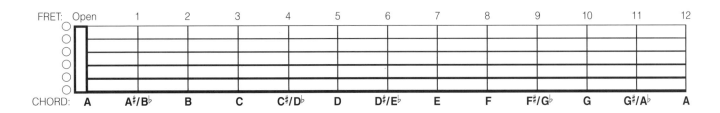

KEY POSITIONS

The I, IV, and V chords in A are A, D, and E, respectively.

TRACK 60

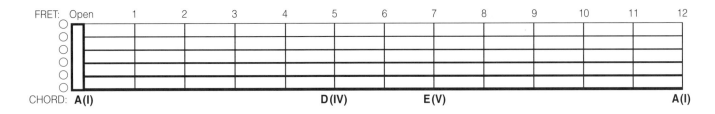

When playing the minor vi chord (F#m) in the key of A, omit the A# note on the second and fifth strings. Rather than trying to keep both strings from ringing, just strum the top four while damping string 2.

TRACK 61

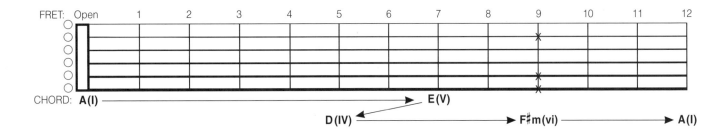

A BLUES

♩ = 86

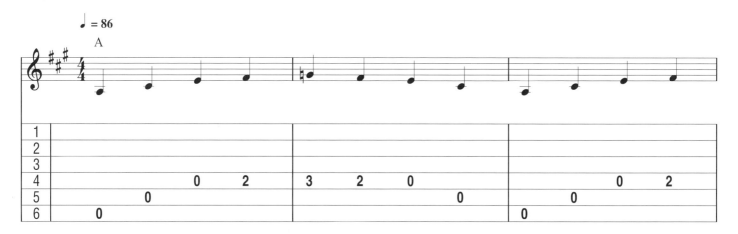

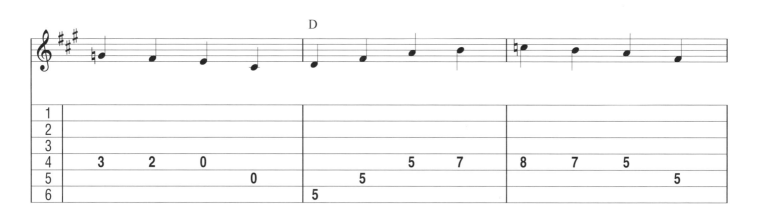

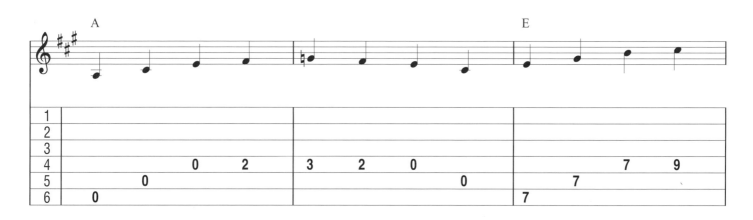

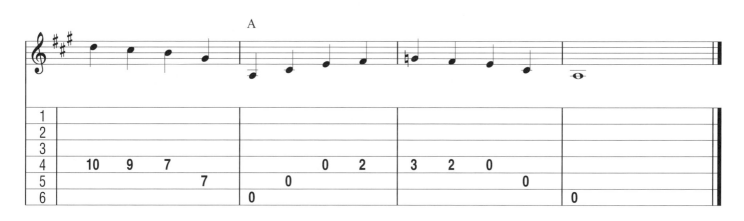

OLD TIME RELIGION

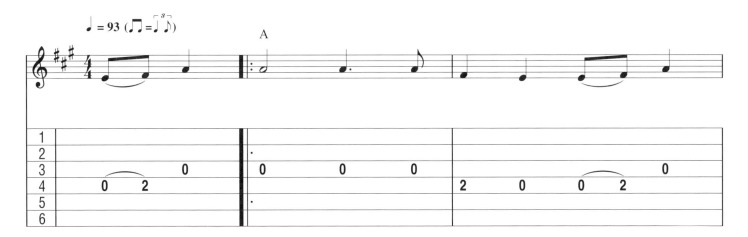

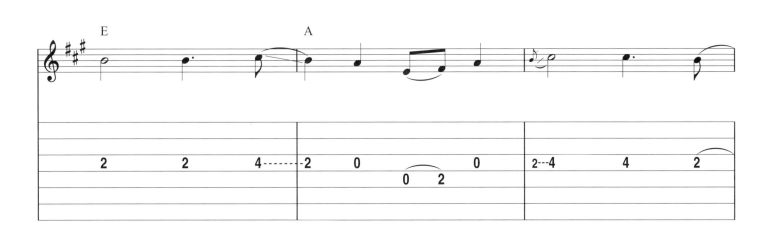

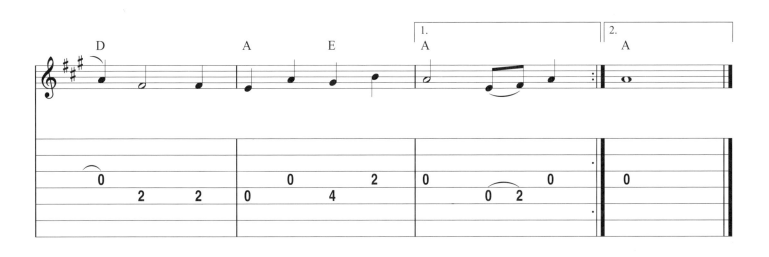

LICKS IN OPEN A

Here are some essential licks in the key of A. When you have learned them, try going back to the rhythm tracks in this chapter and soloing over them using the licks you have learned.

LICK 1

TRACK 66

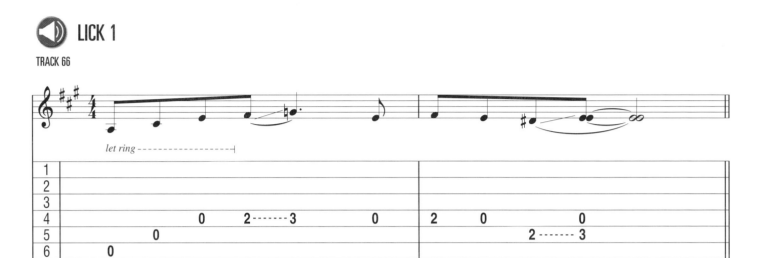

LICK 2

TRACK 67

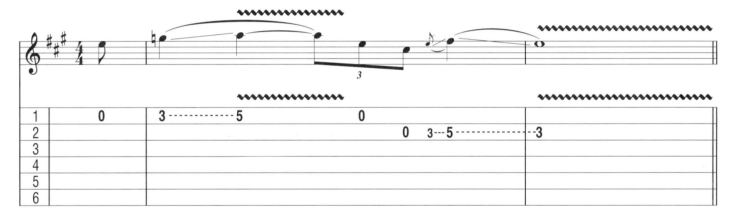

LICK 3

TRACK 68

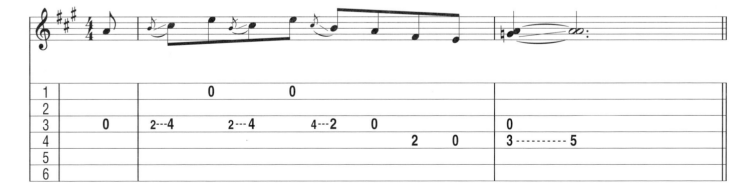

TRACK 69

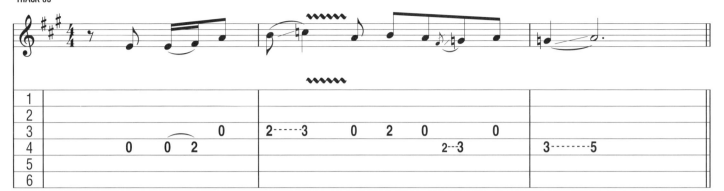

TRACK 70

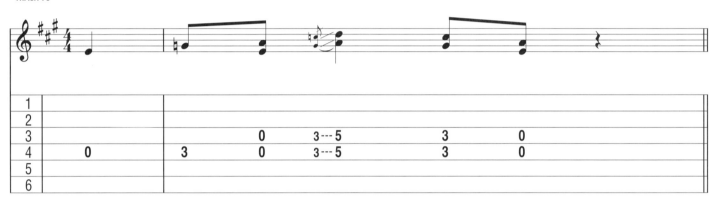

TRACK 71

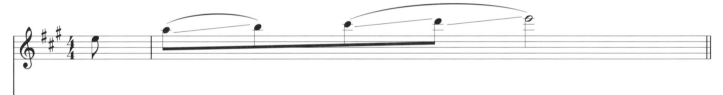

TRACK 72

LICK 8

TRACK 73

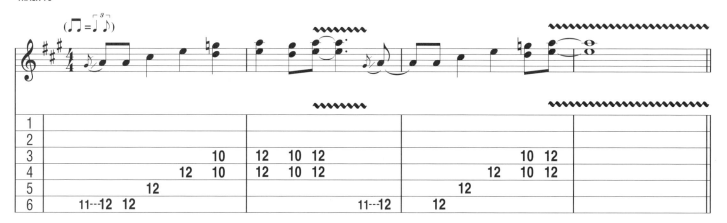

LICK 9

TRACK 74

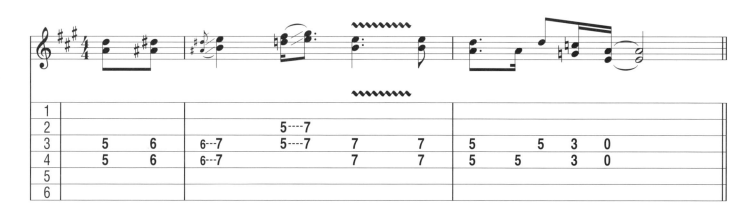

LICK 10

TRACK 75

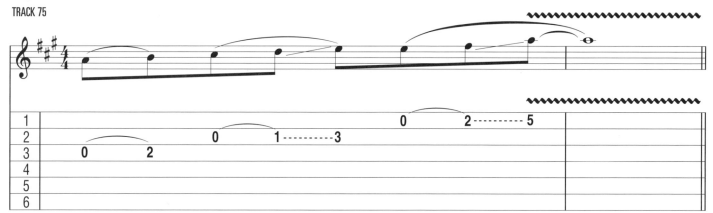

OPEN E TUNING

Here are the notes for open E tuning:

 OPEN E TUNING

TRACK 76

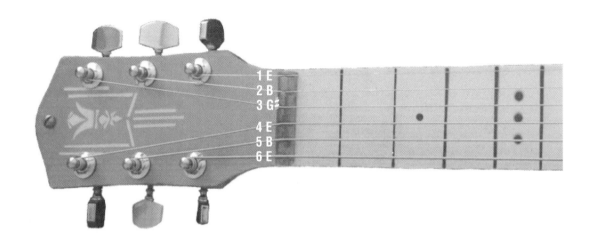

E MAJOR SCALE

 Play along with track 77:
the E major scale in open E tuning.

TRACK 77

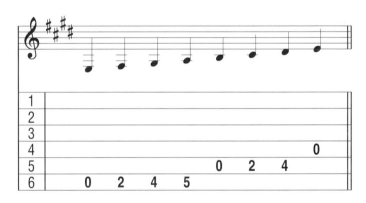

 Track 78 is the E major scale an octave higher.

TRACK 78

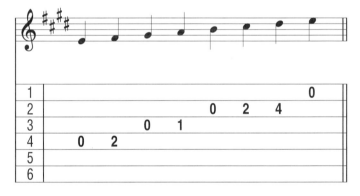

 Track 79 covers both octaves of the E major scale.

TRACK 79

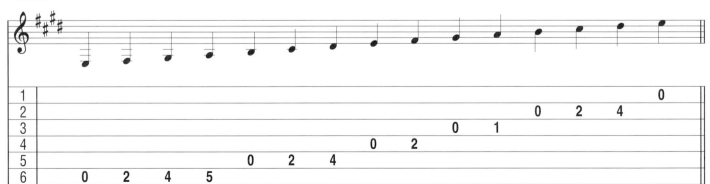

CHORDS IN THE KEY OF E

BASIC MAJOR CHORDS

The open strings in open E tuning form an E major chord with the notes E (the root), G♯ (the 3rd), and B (the 5th). This gives you these major chords across the neck:

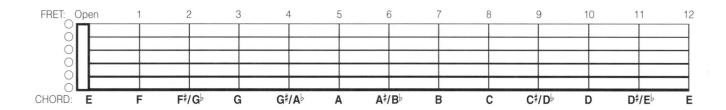

KEY POSITIONS

The I, IV, and V chords in the key of E are E, A, and B.

TRACK 80

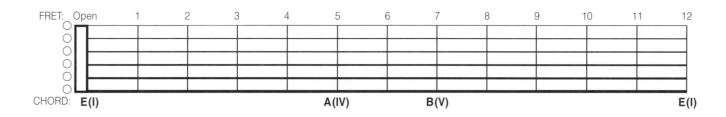

The minor vi chord in the key of E (C♯m) requires you to dampen the third string.

TRACK 81

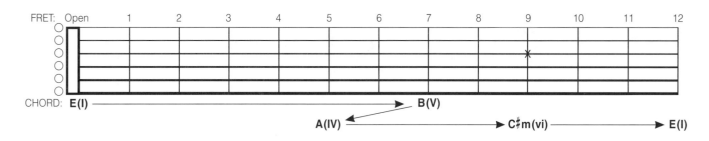

THE STREETS OF LAREDO

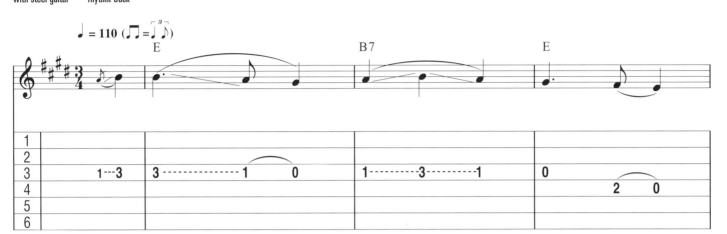

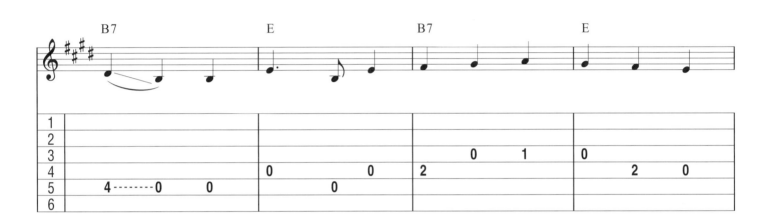

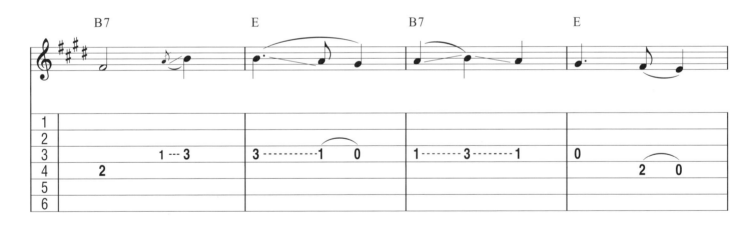

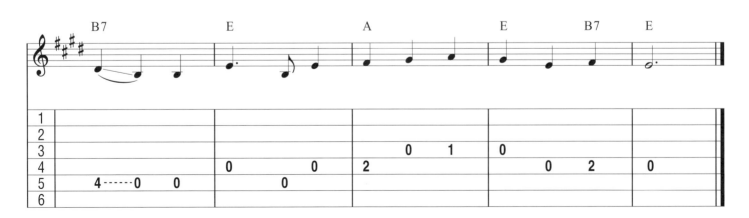

Here's another song in open E tuning. Be sure to play the rakes as indicated throughout.

THE RED RIVER VALLEY

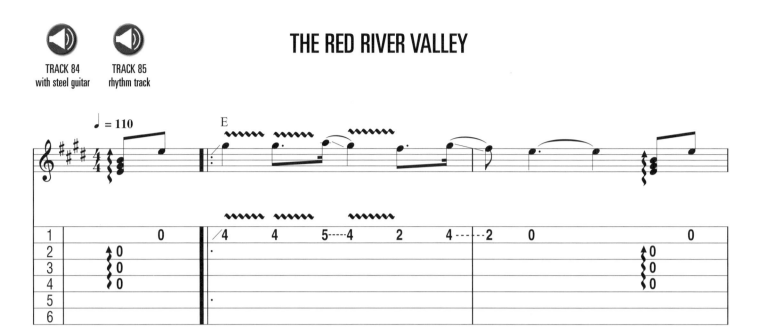

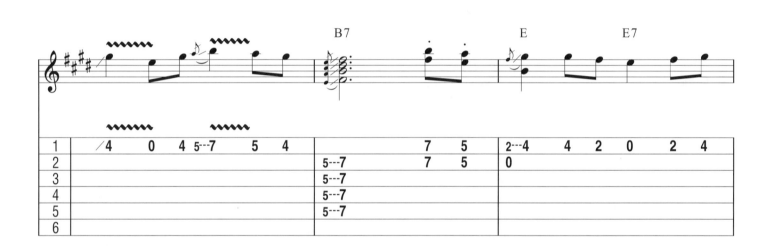

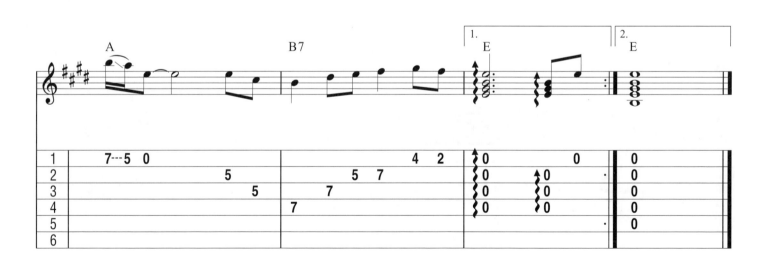

LICKS IN OPEN E

LICK 1

TRACK 86

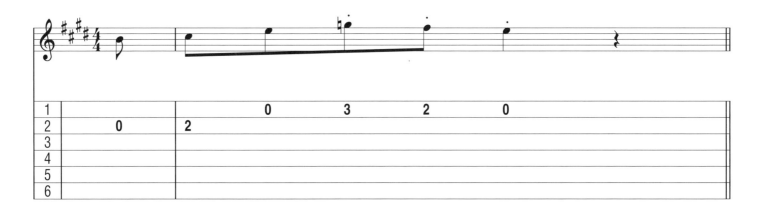

LICK 2

TRACK 87

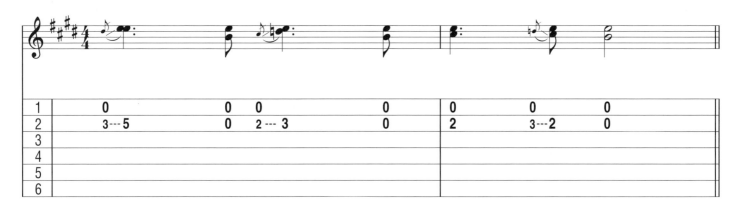

LICK 3

TRACK 88

LICK 4

TRACK 89

LICK 5

TRACK 90

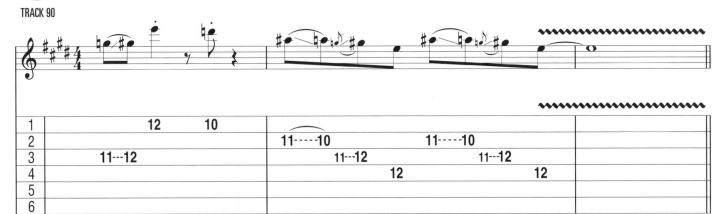

LICK 6

TRACK 91

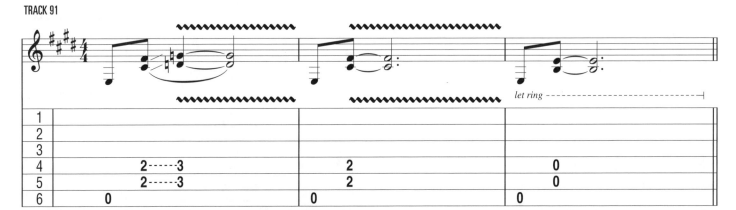

MUTED NOTES

Muted notes are produced by using the blocking or damping technique that we discussed earlier. Damp the strings and pick a note to produce a percussive "click" sound. You'll hear this used in Lick 9.

Another cool technique involving muted notes is called the **rake** (also discussed earlier). While damping the strings, drag your thumb pick across the muted strings quickly, to create a raking sound. Check it out in action in Lick 7!

LICK 7

TRACK 92

LICK 8

TRACK 93

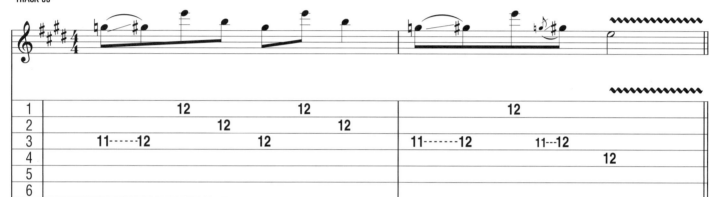

LICK 9

TRACK 94

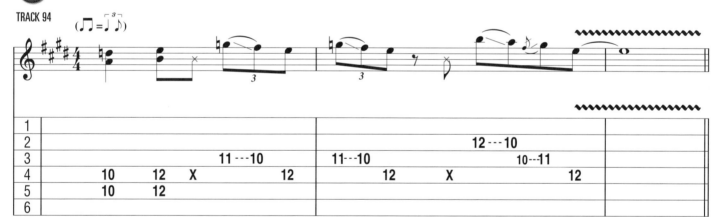

LICK 10

TRACK 95

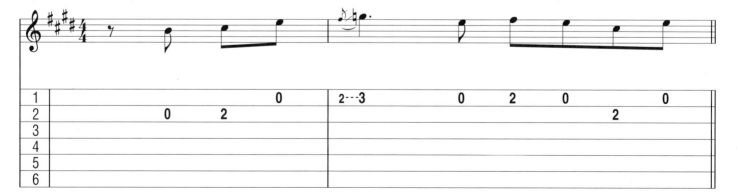

APPENDIX: MUSIC NOTATION

While tablature is great for showing us where to place the bar and which strings to pick on the lap steel, it does not tell us when to play the notes and how long to let them ring out—there's pitch, but no rhythm. This is one reason why we should learn standard notation. Learning to read the same notes that other musicians use also helps us communicate with them better. Here are some basics on music reading.

THE STAFF

Music is written in **notes** on a **staff.** The staff has five lines with four spaces between them. Where a note is written on the staff determines its pitch (highness or lowness). At the beginning of the staff is a **clef sign.** Most melodies are written in the treble clef.

Each line and space of the staff has a letter name. The lines are (from bottom to top) **E–G–B–D–F**, which you can remember as **E**very **G**ood **B**oy **D**oes **F**ine. The spaces are (from bottom to top) **F–A–C–E**, which spells "**Face.**"

The lines and spaces together spell the musical alphabet using the first seven letters of the English alphabet, A through G. Once G is reached, the musical alphabet starts over. Two different notes with the same letter name, for instance E on the first line and E on the fourth space, are said to be an **octave** (eight notes) apart.

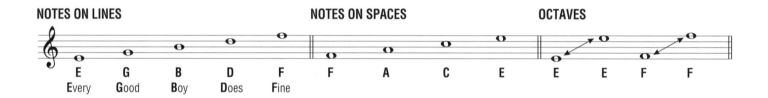

The staff is divided into several parts by **bar lines**. The space between two bar lines is called a **measure** (also known as a "**bar**"). To end a piece of music, a **double bar line** is placed on the staff.

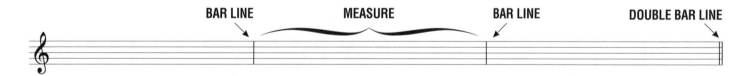

Each measure contains a group of **beats**. Beats are the steady pulse of music. You respond to the pulse or beat when you tap your foot.

TIME SIGNATURE

The top number tells you how many beats are in one measure.
The bottom number tells you what kind of note will receive one beat.

NOTES

Notes indicate the length (number of counts) of a musical sound.

You can tell which pitch to play by the position of a note on the staff, and how long to play it by its shape.

RESTS

In addition to notes, songs may also contain silences—beats in which you play or sing nothing at all. A **rest** is a musical pause. Rests are like notes in that they have their own rhythmic values, instructing you how long (or for how many beats) to pause.

EIGHTH NOTES

If you divide a quarter note in half, you get an **eighth note**. An eighth note looks like a quarter note, but with a flag on its stem.

EIGHTH NOTES

Two eighth notes equal one quarter note. To help you keep track of the beat, consecutive eighth notes are connected with a **beam** instead of having flags.

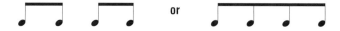

To count eighth notes, divide the beat into two, and use "and" between the beats. Practice this first by counting aloud while tapping your foot on the beat, and then by clapping the notes while counting and foot-tapping.

Eighth rests are counted the same way, but you pause instead of playing.

TIES AND DOTS

The **tie** is a curved line that connects two notes of the same pitch. When you see a tie, play the first note and then hold it for the total value of both notes. Here is an example using a B note.

Ties are useful when you need to extend the value of a note across the bar line.

Another useful way to extend the value of a note is to use a **dot**. A dot extends any note by one-half its value. Most common is the **dotted half note**, which makes it last for three beats. If a measure starts with a dotted half note, then any note written right after if would start on beat 4.

INTERVALS

The smallest distance, or **interval**, between two notes is called a **half step**. If you play any note on your guitar and then play another note one fret higher or lower, you have just played a half step. If you move two frets higher (two half steps up) or two frets lower (two half steps down), you have moved one **whole step**.

ACCIDENTALS

Any note can be raised or lowered in half steps by placing an **accidental** directly before it.

SHARP (♯) ⟶ Raises a note one half step (one fret)
FLAT (♭) ⟶ Lowers a note one half step (one fret)
NATURAL (♮) ⟶ Cancels previously used sharp or flat

LEDGER LINES

Notes higher or lower than the range of the staff are written using ledger lines.

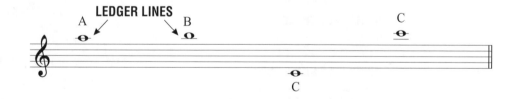

8va

If the notes are so high that ledger lines are hard to read, then the music can be written "*al ottava*," which is Italian for "at the octave," indicated by the symbol **8va** above the staff. The music is then played an octave higher than written.

WRITTEN 8va
BECOMES

HAL LEONARD GUITAR METHOD

METHOD BOOKS, SONGBOOKS AND REFERENCE BOOKS

HAL LEONARD GUITAR METHOD BOOK 1
SECOND EDITION
INCLUDES CD AND ONLINE AUDIO ACCESS
BY WILL SCHMID AND GREG KOCH

THE HAL LEONARD GUITAR METHOD is designed for anyone just learning to play acoustic or electric guitar. It is based on years of teaching guitar students of all ages, and it also reflects some of the best guitar teaching ideas from around the world. This comprehensive method includes: A learning sequence carefully paced with clear instructions; popular songs which increase the incentive to learn to play; versatility – can be used as self-instruction or with a teacher; audio accompaniments so that students have fun and sound great while practicing.

BOOK 1
00699010	Book Only	$8.99
00699027	Book/Online Audio	$12.99
00697341	Book/Online Audio + DVD	$24.99
00697318	DVD Only	$19.99
00155480	Deluxe Beginner Edition (Book, CD, DVD, Online Audio/ Video & Chord Poster)	$19.99

COMPLETE (BOOKS 1, 2 & 3)
00699040	Book Only	$16.99
00697342	Book/Online Audio	$24.99

BOOK 2
00699020	Book Only	$8.99
00697313	Book/Online Audio	$12.99

BOOK 3
00699030	Book Only	$8.99
00697316	Book/Online Audio	$12.99

Prices, contents and availability subject to change without notice.

STYLISTIC METHODS

ACOUSTIC GUITAR
00697347	Method Book/Online Audio	$17.99
00237969	Songbook/Online Audio	$16.99

BLUEGRASS GUITAR
00697405	Method Book/Online Audio	$16.99

BLUES GUITAR
00697326	Method Book/Online Audio (9" x 12")	$16.99
00697344	Method Book/Online Audio (6" x 9")	$15.99
00697385	Songbook/Online Audio (9" x 12")	$14.99
00248636	Kids Method Book/Online Audio	$12.99

BRAZILIAN GUITAR
00697415	Method Book/Online Audio	$17.99

CHRISTIAN GUITAR
00695947	Method Book/Online Audio	$16.99
00697408	Songbook/CD Pack	$14.99

CLASSICAL GUITAR
00697376	Method Book/Online Audio	$15.99

COUNTRY GUITAR
00697337	Method Book/Online Audio	$22.99
00697400	Songbook/Online Audio	$19.99

FINGERSTYLE GUITAR
00697378	Method Book/Online Audio	$21.99
00697432	Songbook/Online Audio	$16.99

FLAMENCO GUITAR
00697363	Method Book/Online Audio	$15.99

FOLK GUITAR
00697414	Method Book/Online Audio	$16.99

JAZZ GUITAR
00695359	Book/Online Audio	$22.99
00697386	Songbook/Online Audio	$15.99

JAZZ-ROCK FUSION
00697387	Book/Online Audio	$24.99

R&B GUITAR
00697356	Book/Online Audio	$19.99
00697433	Songbook/CD Pack	$14.99

ROCK GUITAR
00697319	Book/Online Audio	$16.99
00697383	Songbook/Online Audio	$16.99

ROCKABILLY GUITAR
00697407	Book/Online Audio	$16.99

OTHER METHOD BOOKS

BARITONE GUITAR METHOD
00242055	Book/Online Audio	$12.99

GUITAR FOR KIDS
00865003	Method Book 1/Online Audio	$12.99
00697402	Songbook/Online Audio	$9.99
00128437	Method Book 2/Online Audio	$12.99

MUSIC THEORY FOR GUITARISTS
00695790	Book/Online Audio	$19.99

TENOR GUITAR METHOD
00148330	Book/Online Audio	$12.99

12-STRING GUITAR METHOD
00249528	Book/Online Audio	$19.99

METHOD SUPPLEMENTS

ARPEGGIO FINDER
00697352	6" x 9" Edition	$6.99
00697351	9" x 12" Edition	$9.99

BARRE CHORDS
00697406	Book/Online Audio	$14.99

CHORD, SCALE & ARPEGGIO FINDER
00697410	Book Only	$19.99

GUITAR TECHNIQUES
00697389	Book/Online Audio	$16.99

INCREDIBLE CHORD FINDER
00697200	6" x 9" Edition	$7.99
00697208	9" x 12" Edition	$7.99

INCREDIBLE SCALE FINDER
00695568	6" x 9" Edition	$9.99
00695490	9" x 12" Edition	$9.99

LEAD LICKS
00697345	Book/Online Audio	$10.99

RHYTHM RIFFS
00697346	Book/Online Audio	$14.99

SONGBOOKS

CLASSICAL GUITAR PIECES
00697388	Book/Online Audio	$9.99

EASY POP MELODIES
00697281	Book Only	$7.99
00697440	Book/Online Audio	$14.99

(MORE) EASY POP MELODIES
00697280	Book Only	$6.99
00697269	Book/Online Audio	$14.99

(EVEN MORE) EASY POP MELODIES
00699154	Book Only	$6.99
00697439	Book/Online Audio	$14.99

EASY POP RHYTHMS
00697336	Book Only	$7.99
00697441	Book/Online Audio	$14.99

(MORE) EASY POP RHYTHMS
00697338	Book Only	$7.99
00697322	Book/Online Audio	$14.99

(EVEN MORE) EASY POP RHYTHMS
00697340	Book Only	$7.99
00697323	Book/Online Audio	$14.99

EASY POP CHRISTMAS MELODIES
00697417	Book Only	$9.99
00697416	Book/Online Audio	$14.99

EASY POP CHRISTMAS RHYTHMS
00278177	Book Only	$6.99
00278175	Book/Online Audio	$14.99

EASY SOLO GUITAR PIECES
00110407	Book Only	$9.99

REFERENCE

GUITAR PRACTICE PLANNER
00697401	Book Only	$5.99

GUITAR SETUP & MAINTENANCE
00697427	6" x 9" Edition	$14.99
00697421	9" x 12" Edition	$12.99

For more info, songlists, or to purchase these and more books from your favorite music retailer, go to

halleonard.com

HAL•LEONARD®